M000033430

Encapsulated

poems by

Kristina L. Tregnan

Finishing Line Press
Georgetown, Kentucky

Encapsulated

Copyright © 2019 by Kristina L. Tregnan
ISBN 978-1-63534-838-5 First Edition
All rights reserved under International and Pan-American Copyright Conventions.
No part of this book may be reproduced in any manner whatsoever without written
permission from the publisher, except in the case of brief quotations embodied in
critical articles and reviews.

ACKNOWLEDGMENTS

To my parents Ben and Kathleen, who left this world way too soon, thank you.
Thank you for instilling in me your values and your love of life, for sharing the
importance of family and lifelong friendship. I only wish we had more time
here together. There is not a day that goes by that I do not think of you. xo

To the wonderful physicians and staff at the Marion- Louise Saltzman Women's
Center, Einstein Center One and Einstein Medical Center— Philadelphia, Pa.,
words cannot express my gratitude, Thank You! xo

To Michelle, my family and friends, thank you for your love, your prayers
and your positive thoughts. Without you and your support, I would not have
made it through. How amazingly lucky I am. And to Marianne Defazio, who
we lost this year, you were an inspiration to so many. xo

To Christopher Bursk, how lucky we writers are to have you in our midst.
Without you, this book may never have been a reality. Thank you! xo

Publisher: Leah Maines
Editor: Christen Kincaid
Cover Art and Design: Kristina L. Tregnan
Author Photo: Michele Gerhart

Printed in the USA on acid-free paper.
Order online: www.finishinglinepress.com
also available on amazon.com

Author inquiries and mail orders:
Finishing Line Press
P. O. Box 1626
Georgetown, Kentucky 40324
U. S. A.

Table of Contents

Inside out we are nature at its best.
Conclusions to a long line of cells,
some healthy, some not.
Some of us falling, some of us rising, some of us flying,
some of us just waking up.
Unfurl, listen, move and have a look-see…

1982

The Robin's song
awakens thoughts of my mother...

The clothes calmly blowing
in the breeze
smell of her.
Her telling hands
threading a needle,
peeling potatoes,
or gently stroking my hair
while she lay with me
watching Little House on the Prairie.
She planted sweet mint,
tomatoes, and pink peonies.
The lattice
defining the perimeters
of her genetic garden
passing down the seeds
of sensitivity,
sympathy,
and substance.
My mother finds the cancerous lump
in her breast.
And
spring coming in like a lamb
leaves like a lion.

The Robin's song
awakens thoughts of my mother...

The Diagnostics of Imaging

Creased,
flattened.
The leaf lying still
covers this lazy
earth.
Hiding its salt and minerals
as if to steal them
one by one.
They leach out
rising to the surface.
The wind exposes their growth
like stars
waiting
lined up
pressing against the glass.

The leaf lying still covers this lazy earth. Hiding its salt and minerals as if to steal them one by one.

The Mourning Dove

It was 3:15 pm
as her cell phone
rang
like the whistling of the mourning dove
startled into flight.
The voice
on the other end
spoke softly,
"I have some news for you, is now a good time?"
The mourning dove
already in mid-air
froze,
terrified.
But the sky was still blue
and the other birds still chirped
as if time was still ticking,
but it wasn't.
All the rivers stopped flowing,
all the trees stopped growing,
all the space between her and the earth disappeared.
Nothing but the calming breeze
could help her now.
The threat was imminent,
the repertoire limited,
and all she had were her wings.

Toxic Cravings

The bench is cold.
Cigarette butts litter the dirt
beneath.
They've been there since 1995
faded, wrinkled and yellowed like their owners.
Grabbed by the wind
they float down river
or wiggle their way downstream
on the back of a feather.
Nestled between the rocks
they dip their filters
as the river breathes them in.

The waiting room

The closest chair
holds up her body
bewildered
by the pink ribbon
of novel content.
The words fall asleep
before they reach
the main character
trying to make sense of the
scientific nitty-gritty.
The nuts and bolts
of this tiny cancer
now giving birth inside her.
The steady beat
of this ticking time bomb.

She wishes her feet could fly
return her to yesterday
away from these pastel printed paintings,
these pressed wallflowers
these coffee stained carpets.
Or
fly her to the future
with imprinted imperfections inside
dreaming
of not one but two
reasons
to never wait again.

4:30 a.m.

Cold
slush covered roadway.
Headlights
break the darkness,
as dashes of ice
show themselves.
Thoughts
do not rest,
instead, they float like geese
slowly, steadily, and without notice,
they squawk and fly out of sight.
The distance becomes less
and less,
as the butterflies panic into a cold sweat.
The gate lifts
at 5:45am.
A wintry hand touches mine
offering warmth and reassurance.
But none
will be found
today.

Blue

Feeling the pin prick
of the needle
she floated off
into fiction.
The hands she was in,
wrinkled and wise,
removed the quiet stars
determined to lift off
and spread like this centuries-old disease.
The knowing blue dye injected
traveled
as if it was a detective in the 35th district
looking for the highwayman.
But the search came up empty.
No stars, no broken cells traveled these
veiny routes.
Relieved
she awakens in bed 4.
Blue
but breathing and blessed.

Encapsulated

How calm they are
these delicate stars inside
communicating
whispering about their distance.
They could cover more ground
multiply into groups of three or more
if time was on their side.
Wait!
They have been found
hiding within the lobules
sneaking quietly through the ducts
like a gunman in search of his five minutes of fame.
A hypocritical silence
dances around organic farm fresh
vs conventional.
Truth vs lies.
Health moves forward no longer skeptical of the soil.
A hand reaches in and cuts through the margins,
removed.

Uninhabitable

The metallicness of it
sends a shiver.
Reflections shine
but the sun
has never shown itself here.
Crisp white sheets
layer the flat stretcher,
smell of cancer causing chemicals.
Silence is lost in between
the beeping call bells
and
the whistling
heart monitors.
Nausea arrives at the front door
impatiently waiting to
take out the trash.
She sits up slightly
stretches her legs.
Her stomach cleans itself
of the anesthesia.
Closing her eyes
she lies back
thanking God
that it's over.
She doesn't think
she could do it
again.

The Infection

The wind blew that day.
Struggling to lift herself
from these roots attached to her
like a Sunday afternoon,
she lifted her breast
and a river found its way
out.
Towels fell to the floor,
they jumped to their death,
desperately sopping up the rotten red and white blood cells.
The pressing quickened
until the river had emptied.
The cleaning up
dipped into the DNA
and found the sickness.
The second skin
rested behind the surgical tape.
Her breath settled down
to wind between the trees
and thank god
the leaves
hung on.

The Uncertainties

In front of the sun
the trees
show off their curves
and sway
as the wind combs through their leaves.
The open window
doesn't hesitate to introduce
this slumberous scene.
The remainder of the day
sits quietly
as she waits,
curled up on the couch
for the noise of the telephone.
A flood of light and vibration
breaks up the energy.
Moving forward
she gently says, "Hello"
The voice on the other end
kindly says, "Your test results reveal,
no chemo needed!"
Words form into quick jolts of elation and one long *YESsssss*.

*The rhythm of the woodpecker pecking, the white throated sparrow whispering
soft and slow, the sound of leaves crinkling quickly across the dried dirt
carried by a spirited breeze.*
These things matter.

The Sense and the Sensibility

The birds chirp
as if nothing has happened.
Can't they see the dichotomy between the sense and the sensibility?
The brutal grasp of reality vs. the imaginative fiction?
There is a fine line resting on a ridge and crossing the chest
Tattooed.
Its purpose is related to precision.
It spins and spins
until it rests upon the center of its target.
Stillness is of utmost importance
numbness follows
filling the hands first
reaching down through the arms.
"Rest assured,"
said the sensibility,
it's almost over
but

the sense

knows better.

These Things Matter

The billowing bright rhododendron,
the honeysuckle,
    the lilacs.
The feel of pebbles softened
       from the roaring river
rolling between your toes.
These things matter.

The rhythm of the woodpecker pecking,
the white throated sparrow whispering
    soft and slow,
the sound of leaves crinkling quickly
       across the dried dirt
carried by a spirited breeze.
These things matter.

The moment when you comprehend
       the lesson,
the questions you have,
    the options you have,
       the answers arriving
as unforgettable songs,
   reminding you to remember,
These things matter.

Bring to Light

The silkworm
in delicate circles
spinning its way
into a cocoon
with edges
masterfully
concealing
its growth.
Webs weave
in and out
under and over.

The spotlight
of a helicopter
searches
jiggling the ground
as the light passes
through the gravel.
There's no sign
of the intruder
hiding in the mulberry trees.

In the darkroom
the Radiologist
leans forward in her chair
placing the magnifier
against
the complicated clouds of
tissue
compressed
captured
black and white.
Silently,
swiftly,
she saves my life.

Wishes and Prayers

Gathering
against the grain
she tosses her
handmade
handkerchief
into the wishing well.
A sacrifice
for the Gods.
Her prayers
reach up through the sunset.
There is little time
ahead
of this world in front of her now.
These poisoned pills
take away
one diseased cell
for another
yet,
there's no victory.
Wincing at the sunlight
her worrisome premonition
waits for a revelation
thanking God
before tomorrow
comes.

Morning Walk

The gray catbird
mews and kwuts
flipping over leaves
searching
for the dogbane leaf beetle.
Asymmetrical shadows
letting the light in
sway
to the rhythm of the forest floor.
Morning dew
clings
from long slivers of bright green grass
Breathing in the sweet smell
of wild honeysuckle
she steps a little slower
reminiscing over the honey-like
drop
suspended
waiting
at the tip of the flower.

Breathing in the sweet smell of wild honeysuckle she steps a little slower reminiscing over the honey-like drop suspended waiting at the tip of the flower.

Intangible

A drop here
on a leaf

A drop there
on the dried dirt.

A cold damp spring
rain
yet, she remains
sitting on her bench
accepting the cleansing raindrops
as she faces the cloudy
sky.
The world will not end
as a result of her wet hair.

Little worries her now.
She's found a place of perspective
that removes
the incidentals.
She wishes she made more money
of course.
Other than that, she recognizes
she has everything
she needs.

She unfurls

The birch leaves
curled up in their cocoons
listen
for their moment
to let loose
and
unfurl.

Still there is a chill
to the spring air
wrestling
with winter for change.

She counts
the days
crossing them off
craving the scent
of cut grass
and lemonade on her lips.

On the surface
the scars
now faded
carry with them
a token of her
time with cancer.

Listening
for her moment
to let loose,
she
Unfurls.

Purpose

The uninterested river
exposes the silence.
The moss covered rocks
struggle to interrupt
as the sun bathing fly
utilizes their warmth.
The wind brushes by
making way for restoration.
Instigated by her burnt breast
she moves in the direction
of premeditated planting
arranges the angles
leaving way for discussion, advice
and growth.
The shift
stretches the intentions
across her senses.
The sky
clear
let's her know
the river too
is listening.

Renovate

I turn the page.
Ahead there is work to be done

Solid change
intermingles with hesitation.

How?

To move forward
don't wait
step and then step again.

Inside the words form,

Listen.

Closely.
Carefully.

Turn the page.

…And breathe

The science
nestles in there
between the cold clear plastic
and her long lost modesty.
In minutes,
it only takes minutes
to reveal
these broken cells
clumped together
hitching a ride on the back of a distorted Ferris wheel.
But the fun is over.
The ride jerks forward
then back
squeaking
softly.
The room is small
with two doors
one to go in
one to go out.
The button down half shirt
flatters no one
waiting for this type of disclosure.
Fingers and hands gently rest
on her faded jeans,
sweaty.
The in door
opens,
and the broken cells
have nowhere
left to go but out.

The Horizon

Taking a look outward
I fumble,
working towards
some sort of middle.
The ground
gives way every now and again.
My surroundings
less and less tolerable.

The push
comes from behind.
Moving this sedentary
situation aside,
the branches point north.
Patience is waiting
across the street,
silent again.

I press the keyboard
answer the phone,
as another day sets itself.

The dark drive home
I dwell on the light.
The push
comes from behind again.
Listening,
I lean forward.

All Natural

Craving
the sound of the Eastern Meadowlark,
she walked into the woods.
The air was cool
for a late August morning.
The ring and rattle
of the summer locusts
commanded
all the attention.
Breathing in the freshness
of 8 a.m.,
she stepped forward
and stretched her arms above her head.
She wanted to stroll the crooked trail
into a much cheaper
addiction.
To be
in this place
only,
right here
in between
the ash tree and the pine,
the oak and the birch.

She talks to trees

There is no hesitation
within the silent
chatter
she shares among
the Sugar Maple.

A gentle breeze
wakes up
its pointy leaves.

The birds interrupt
calling for their kin.

The fallen acorn
reveals
its secrets.

The Neshaminy Creek
casually drifts by.

No hurry, no place to be,
she sits quietly
listening
for her directions.

Into the Woods, I Go

I breath in
the sweet scent of the soil
beneath my feet.

The soft sun of September
warms the morning chill
from the delicate green leaves
of the Lady Fern.

The grey squirrel
stirs to the call of
the White-Throated Sparrow.

Tiny tinkering of bells
from the ground cricket
carry their echo
from north to south, east to west.

I listen quietly

The leaves crinkle
beneath my feet,
and create a corridor
of reds, yellows and orange.

My lens lingers long enough
to capture
the bend in the breeze.
It lifts up the leaves

and carries them into winter.

1:11

One new beginning
finds me,

reaching
　　　for my pen.

Letting go
　　　of certainty,

finding movement
in the right direction,

for this too
may go away.

As balance finds itself
immeasurable

there is that drop
of water

　　　a constant

that always brings
ripples.

As balance finds itself immeasurable there is that drop of water a constant that always brings ripples.

Kristina Tregnan is a writer, photographer, and graphic designer living in beautiful Bucks County, Pa. She has studied poetry and creative writing and has also received her Graphic Design degree and a certificate in Applied Photography from Bucks County Community College, Newtown, Pa. Kristina works full time at Einstein Medical Center, Philadelphia, Pa. She enjoys spending her days off outdoors and can be found walking the trails of Tyler State Park, photographing nature, wild life and landscapes or writing at her favorite bench overlooking the Neshaminy Creek.

CPSIA information can be obtained
at www.ICGtesting.com
Printed in the USA
LVHW041916190419
614903LV00001B/31/P